Introduction

Redwork became popular in the late 1800s when Turkey red thread was used for embroidery. The red thread was colorfast, unlike other colors of the time, and called Turkey red because it originated in Turkey. Redwork designs were embroidered using a simple outline stitch, so they often were used by young girls who were learning to embroider. Today, the simplicity of embroidery done all in one color has become popular once again. You do not have to limit yourself to only Turkey red. Feel free to use any shade of red; simply pick the color that enhances the fabric you are using.

Sunbonnet Sue patterns became popular in the early 1900s. Drawn by artists such as Kate Greenaway and Bertha Corbett, these designs were often used for redwork embroidery. The designs in this book were inspired by Bertha Corbett's style of "Sunbonnet Babies" (she illustrated a book by the same name) that captured the sweet innocence of youth. The following pages take Sunbonnet Sue, stitched all in red, through the seasons and holidays. She has not lost her charm with age, and she delights both young and old. Redwork embroidery is the ideal take-along project for the busy lives we now lead.

For your convenience, we have included these Sunbonnet Sue embroidery designs for you to trace or transfer—you can choose which method you prefer. The tracing designs are given first, and the transfer designs follow on iron-on transfer pages.

Enjoy!

Meet the Designer

Loyce Saxton has been designing embroidery patterns for the past 16 years. She lives with her husband in Oregon, where she was born and raised, and she loves the mountains and trees that surround her home. The ladies of her family have sewed for generations, and when Loyce was a little girl, her mother would bring out a box of thread, buttons, fabric, beads, felt, pins and needles, and just let her play. Most of what she made were doll clothes. She has been sewing since then. She has not only made quilts, but she sewed clothes for herself and for her children. If she's sewing, she's happy.

As a wife and mother of three she kept busy with family life until the children were almost grown. Then, with nobody to sew for, she began Yesterday's Charm, a pattern company specializing in hand embroidery and quilting patterns. She was always encouraged to be creative, and the sewing treasures of her mother's are now hers. Those sewing-room treasures were the inspiration for her business. She is always inspired by the past and is constantly searching for new and fresh ideas. You can see her full collection of patterns online at www.yesterdayscharm.com.

 DISCLAIMER: The items in this book should be washed two or three times to ensure that the iron-on inks do not irritate the skin, especially for babies and children.

 Sunbonnet Sue Redwork Collection for All Seasons is published by Annie's, 306 East Parr Road, Berne, IN 46711. Printed in USA. Copyright © 2014, 2018 Annie's. All rights reserved. This publication may not be reproduced in part or in whole without written permission from the publisher.

RETAIL STORES: If you would like to carry this publication or any other Annie's publication, visit AnniesWSL.com.

Every effort has been made to ensure that the instructions in this publication are complete and accurate. We cannot, however, take responsibility for human error, typographical mistakes or variations in individual work. Please visit AnniesCustomerService.com to check for pattern updates.

ISBN: 978-1-57367-573-4   Library of Congress Control Number: 2015934023   7 8 9 10 11 12

Table of Contents

Redwork Basics

Redwork embroidery requires a few supplies and some simple instructions. Take a moment to become acquainted with these basic instructions and stitches before beginning your projects.

Supplies

Fabric

If you can get your needle and floss through the fabric, you can embroider it. However, a nice-quality fabric is a good choice if you want your work to last. Pre-washing is a good idea if your fabric is going to be washed regularly; otherwise it is not necessary.

Embroidery Floss

Six-strand cotton embroidery floss was used to embroider the designs in these redwork projects. Each project lists the specific Cosmo color used by the designer and a comparable DMC color. All the embroidery was done using two strands of floss that were cut in about 26-inch lengths. The strands of floss are pulled out one at a time then brought together to thread the needle and stitch. Be sure the floss you use is guaranteed to be colorfast.

Embroidery Hoops

The best embroidery results are often achieved when using an embroidery hoop to hold the fabric taut while stitching. However the choice is yours whether to hoop or not to hoop.

Redwork Embroidery

There are two methods of transferring the embroidery designs to your fabric. The designs given for tracing show the right side while the designs for iron-on transfer are reversed.

Tracing the Design

Cut fabric to be embroidered into the size specified with each project's instructions.

Center the fabric over the printed design and trace, using a sharp lead pencil or fabric marking pen or pencil. If you use a fabric pen, be sure to follow the manufacturer's directions for proper use. If you cannot see the design lines clearly, use a light box for tracing. Remember that the traced lines should not be visible on the finished project.

Iron-On Transferring the Design

1. Cut out the printed design, trimming away anything you do not want transferred to the fabric.

2. Place a piece of plain paper on the ironing board to protect it from any bleed through. Iron your fabric flat where you will be transferring the design.

3. Lay the design used for transferring print side down onto the fabric and center it.

4. Use a dry iron on the hottest setting and iron slowly, moving back and forth, and holding the paper still for 10 to 15 seconds.

5. Holding the design in place, carefully lift up a corner to make sure the design transferred to the fabric. If it did not transfer, keep ironing until it completely transfers. If you remove the transfer and there are incomplete lines or lines that are not dark enough, go back over the design lines with a sharp lead pencil or fabric pen.

Embroidering the Design

You can start and stop your stitching with a knot, or you can weave the floss in between the stitches on the back side. On the back side, try not to cross over a large area; the floss will show through on the finished project. When stitching is completed, press face-down on a terry towel to finish.

Stitch Guide

Follow these detailed instructions and stitch diagrams, and refer to the embroidery designs and photos of the projects to stitch them like the samples.

Outline Stitch

The outline stitch is used for solid lines.

For the outline stitch, bring the needle and thread up at 1 and insert the needle at 2. Keeping the thread below the needle, bring the needle back up at 3 (halfway between 1 and 2). Insert the needle at 4 and bring it back out near the hole for 2. Continue on the line, always bringing the needle out in the hole of the previous stitch.

Outline Stitch

Lazy Daisy Stitch

The lazy daisy stitch is used to make flower petals or small leaves. If you leave the stitches loose, you will make wider loops; if you pull the stitches tighter, you will have straighter, thinner loops.

Bring the needle and thread up at 1. Holding the thread down with the thumb of your non-needle hand, insert the needle into 2, next to 1, and come up at 3, over the loop of thread. Insert the needle directly above 3 at 4 to secure and complete the stitch.

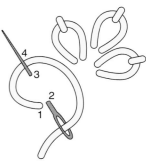

Lazy Daisy Stitch

Fly Stitch

The fly stitch is used to stitch any U-shape, which works well to make little fingers or flower petals when not using lazy daisy stitches.

Bring the needle and thread up at 1 and insert at 2, directly across from 1. Bring the needle back up at 3, below and centered between 1 and 2. Take the needle down at 4 to finish the stitch.

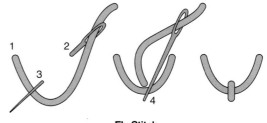

Fly Stitch

Running Stitch

The running stitch is used to stitch dashed lines.

Run the needle in and out of the fabric at regular intervals.

Running Stitch

French Knot

French knots are fun, dimensional stitches often used for dots, eyes and flower centers. French knots are shown as filled-in black dots on the embroidery designs.

To make a French knot, bring the needle and thread up at 1. Hold the thread taut and wrap it around the needle once; then pull it gently to keep the wrap snug but not too tight. Keeping the tension, insert the needle back into the fabric at 2, about one thread away from 1. Push the loop down the needle to lie on top of the fabric, and then pull the needle through carefully.

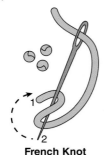

French Knot

Cross Stitch

The cross stitch is used to stitch all X's.

Bring the needle and thread up at 1. Take a diagonal stitch down at 2 and come up at 3. Take a diagonal stitch back down at 4.

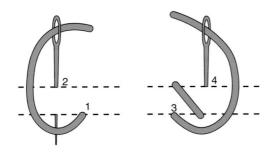

Single Cross-Stitch

Satin Stitch

The satin stitch is a stitch used to fill a shape completely without leaving spaces. It consists of straight stitches worked side by side, closely together.

Start at one side of the motif and bring the needle up at 1. Take the stitch back down at 2, across the shape. Come up again at 3, a thread or two away from 1, to make the next stitch. Take the stitches across from side to side, keeping them even and close together. This stitch can be made horizontally, vertically or diagonally.

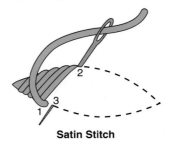

Satin Stitch

Star Stitch

The star stitch is a variation of the cross stitch and is used to stitch stars.

Bring the needle and thread up at 1. Take a diagonal stitch down at 2 and come up at 3. Take a diagonal stitch back down at 4 and come up at 5. Make a final stitch to 6 to form a star. ●

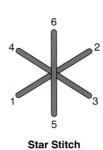

Star Stitch

The Four Seasons

A framed set of the four seasons will brighten a wall all year long.

Finished Size
12 x 10 inches

Materials
- 1 yard white solid
- 1 yard bleached muslin
- Red embroidery floss (Cosmo #346 or DMC #321)
- 8 (10-inch) stretcher bars
- 8 (12-inch) stretcher bars
- Staple gun
- Basic sewing tools and supplies

Cutting

From white solid:
- Cut 4 (16 x 14-inch) rectangles.

From bleached muslin:
- Cut 4 (16 x 14-inch) rectangles.

The Four Seasons
Placement Diagram 12" x 10"

Embroidery

1. Iron-on transfer or trace the spring, autumn, summer and winter embroidery designs in the center of each white solid rectangle.

2. Embroider using two strands of floss, referring to Redwork Basics on page 3 as needed.

3. Press facedown on a terry towel to finish.

Assembly

After stitching has been completed, you may prefer to take your stitched pieces to a framer, or you can frame them yourself using stretcher bars and following these instructions.

1. Lay each embroidered rectangle facedown with a muslin rectangle on top and iron out any wrinkles. Trim edges of muslin rectangles even with the embroidered rectangles if necessary.

2. Assemble stretcher bars to form four 12 x 10-inch frames following manufacturer's instructions.

3. Center each stretcher bar frame on the muslin and trim off the muslin corners to reduce bulk.

4. Wrap the two layers of fabric around the top bar and staple in place on the inside edge of the top bar.

5. Wrap the fabric snugly around the bottom bar and staple in place.

6. Pull sides around snugly and staple once on the inside edge in the center of each side.

7. Tuck the corners in so the fold of each corner lines up with each corner and finish stapling. ●

Spring Pillow

These rickrack flowers look good for spring, summer or fall since flowers grow through these seasons. For winter, make them white to look like snowballs.

Finished Size
16 x 12 inches

Materials
- ⅛ yard red tonal
- ½ yard white tonal
- Red embroidery floss (Cosmo #242 or DMC #498)
- ⅔ yard 1⅜-inch-wide red rickrack
- 1⅓ yards ⅝-inch-wide red rickrack
- 16 x 12-inch pillow form
- Thread
- Safety pins (optional)
- Basic sewing tools and supplies

Cutting

From red tonal:
- Cut 2 (1⅛ x 25¼-inch) strips.

From white tonal:
- Cut 2 (17¼ x 13¼-inch) rectangles.

Embroidery
1. Iron-on transfer or trace the spring embroidery design in the center of one white rectangle.

2. Embroider using two strands of floss, referring to Redwork Basics on page 3 as needed.

3. Press facedown on a terry towel to finish.

Assembly
Stitch right sides together using a ⅝-inch seam allowance unless otherwise indicated.

1. Place embroidered pillow front right sides together with second white rectangle; trim edges even, if necessary. Sew the top seam only. Press seam toward the back rectangle.

2. Press under ¼ inch on both long edges of the red tonal strips. With front and back right sides facing up, position strips 2½ inches away from each long side of the pillow and machine-topstitch in place as shown in Figure 1.

Figure 1

3. Fold the pillow cover along seam with right sides facing and finish stitching the remaining sides leaving an 8-inch opening for turning along the bottom.

4. Turn cover right side out and insert pillow form. Hand-stitch opening closed using a blind stitch.

Large Rickrack Flower

1. Cut a 20-inch length of 1⅜-inch rickrack and then fold in half lengthwise.

2. Baste along the folded edge as shown in Figure 2. Gather up tightly and knot.

Figure 2

3. Fold over one end and start rolling up the rickrack, securing with stitches as you roll it as shown in Figure 3.

Figure 3

4. When you finish rolling, wrap the other cut end to the underside of the flower and stitch in place as shown in Figure 4.

Figure 4

5. Trim loose ends and spread out the petals.

6. Attach to pillow with a safety pin so it can easily be removed when the pillow is washed, or hand-stitch in place.

Small Rickrack Flowers

1. Cut a 20-inch length of ⅝-inch rickrack. Fold the strip in half and weave together as shown in Figure 5.

Figure 5

2. Starting at the folded end with a good knot, baste through the lower humps of the rickrack as shown in Figure 6. Gather tightly and knot.

Figure 6

3. Fold down the cut end and start rolling the rickrack, stitching it in place as you go and ending with the folded end. Finish with a knot.

4. Trim away any loose ends.

5. Repeat steps 1–4 for the second small flower.

6. Attach both small flowers to pillow with safety pins so they can easily be removed when the pillow is washed, or hand-stitch in place. ●

Spring Pillow
Placement Diagram 16" x 12"

Easter Towels

Bring some holiday cheer to your kitchen by stitching up a set of towels. These towels also make a great hostess gift.

Finished Size
Size varies

Materials
- 3 purchased towels
- ¼ yard each three red prints
- Red embroidery floss (Cosmo #346 or #DMC 321)
- 3 yards ⅝-inch-wide tan rickrack
- Thread
- Basic sewing tools and supplies

Cutting

From each red print:
- Cut 1 (3½" x 27½-inch) strip (or the width of the towel plus ½ inch).

Embroidery

1. Iron-on transfer or trace bunnies, bird and Easter eggs embroidery designs in the center of each towel 4½ inches from the bottom edge.

2. Embroider using two strands of floss, referring to Redwork Basics on page 3 as needed. *Note: Bird and bunny eyes were satin stitched on sample.*

3. Press facedown on a terry towel to finish.

Assembly

1. Press under ¼ inch on all edges of each red print strip.

2. Position a red print strip along bottom of each towel and pin in place matching ends of the fabric with the towel side edges.

3. Cut rickrack into three 29-inch lengths (or the width of your towel plus 2 inches). Tuck the rickrack halfway under the top of the fabric edge with end of rickrack extending an inch on either end as shown in Figure 1. Pin in place.

Figure 1

4. Machine-topstitch the fabric edge all the way around, about 1/16 inch from the edge.

5. Wrap the raw edge of the rickrack around to the back side and machine-stitch 1/4 inch from the edge.

6. Trim off the excess rickrack 1/4 inch from the stitching.

7. Referring to the photo on page 13, stitch a French knot to the center of each "hill" of the rickrack using three strands of floss. ●

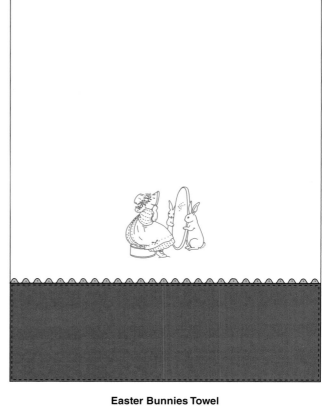

Easter Bunnies Towel
Placement Diagram Size Varies

Easter Eggs Towel
Placement Diagram Size Varies

Easter Bird Towel
Placement Diagram Size Varies

Summer Tray

Serve up the treats of the season on this useful tray.
Stitch tray cloths for spring, autumn and winter
as well, and switch them as the seasons change.

Finished Size

Size varies

Materials

- ⅜ yard white solid
- Red embroidery floss (Cosmo #346
  or DMC #321)
- Tray at least 11 x 7½ inches with glass inset
- Thread
- Basic sewing tools and supplies

Cutting

From white solid:

- Cut 1 (12 x 8½-inch) rectangle (or the size of the
  bottom inside of tray plus 1" in both directions).

Embroidery

1. Iron-on transfer or trace the summer embroidery
design in the center of the white solid rectangle.

2. Embroider using two strands of floss, referring to
Redwork Basics on page 3 as needed.

3. Press facedown on a terry towel to finish.

Assembly

1. Fold and press edges ¼ inch to the wrong side and
then ¼ inch again; machine-topstitch to complete a
double-turned hem.

2. Place completed cloth in tray and top with the
glass inset. ●

Summer Tray
Placement Diagram Size Varies

Halloween Pennant Banner

This Sunbonnet Sue banner will liven up your autumn decor and is a great way to use those holiday fabrics you've been collecting.

Finished Size
87 x 10 inches

Materials
- ½ yard white tonal
- 3 orange print fat quarters
- 3 black print fat quarters
- Red embroidery floss (Cosmo #242 or DMC #498)
- 3 yards black extra-wide double-fold bias tape
- 2 yards ¼-inch-wide black rickrack
- Thread
- Basic sewing tools and supplies

Cutting

From white tonal:
- Cut 6 pennants using pattern provided.

From orange prints:
- Cut 2 pennants from each orange print using pattern provided.

From black prints:
- Cut 2 pennants from each black print using pattern provided.

Embroidery

1. Iron-on transfer or trace the pumpkin carving, Halloween cat and scary Halloween embroidery designs in the center of three white pennants.

2. Embroider using two strands of floss, referring to Redwork Basics on page 3 as needed.

3. Press facedown on a terry towel to finish.

Assembly

Machine-stitch with right sides together using a ¼-inch seam allowance.

1. Cut a 23-inch length of rickrack. On an embroidered pennant, center rickrack along the seam line on the two angled sides and baste in place as shown in Figure 1. Trim ends of rickrack even with top edge of pennant.

Figure 1

2. With right sides together sew a plain white pennant to embroidered pennant around both sides leaving the top open.

3. Trim bottom point, turn right side out and press flat.

4. Repeat steps 1–3 to make a total of 3 white embroidered pennants.

5. Repeat steps 2 and 3 to make 3 orange and 3 black pennants.

6. Arrange pennants in the order you wish or as shown in Placement Diagram. Pin the top corners together, overlapping ⅝-inch as shown in Figure 2.

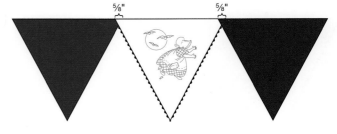

Figure 2

7. Position and pin the top edge of the banner into the fold of the bias tape leaving 11" on each end for ties. Stitch along length and across ends of bias tape using a zigzag stitch. ●

Halloween Pennant Banner
Placement Diagram 87" x 10"

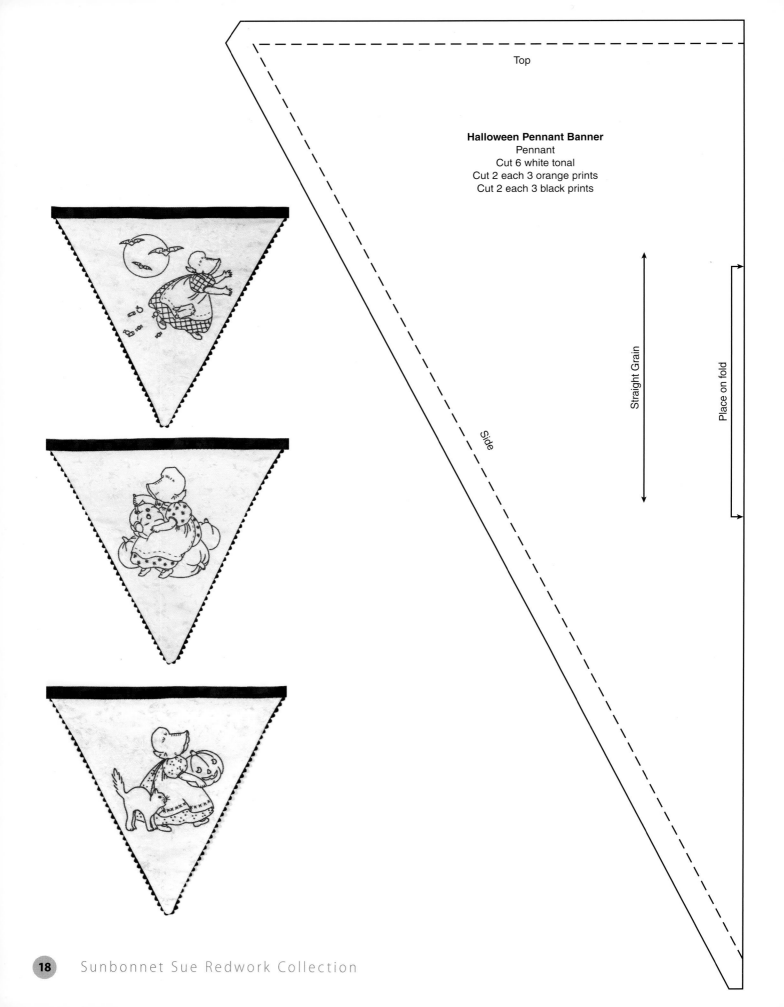

Halloween Pennant Banner
Pennant
Cut 6 white tonal
Cut 2 each 3 orange prints
Cut 2 each 3 black prints

Top

Side

Straight Grain

Place on fold

Thanksgiving Hot Pads

When things heat up in the kitchen, grab Sunbonnet Sue for the rescue.

Finished Size
8 x 8 inches (includes binding)

Materials
- ⅜ yard cream tonal
- ⅝ yard autumn print
- Red embroidery floss (Cosmo #2241 or DMC #816)
- 9 x 18-inch rectangle needle-punched insulating batting
- Thread
- Basic sewing tools and supplies

Cutting

From cream tonal:
- Cut 2 (9-inch) A squares.

From autumn print:
- Cut 2 (1½-inch by fabric width) strips.
  Subcut strips into 4 (1½ x 6-inch) B borders and 4 (1½ x 8-inch) C borders.
- Cut 2 (2¼-inch by fabric width) strips for binding.
- Cut 2 (9-inch) backing squares.

From needle-punched insulating batting:
- Cut 2 (9-inch) squares.

Embroidery

1. Iron-on transfer or trace the feeding turkey and turkey dinner embroidery designs in the center of A squares.

2. Embroider using two strands of floss, referring to Redwork Basics on page 3 as needed.

3. Press facedown on a terry towel to finish and trim each to a 6-inch square.

Assembly
Machine-stitch with right sides together using a ¼-inch seam allowance.

1. Sew a B border to the top and bottom of an embroidered A square as shown in Figure 1. Press seams toward borders.

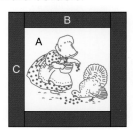

Figure 1

2. Sew a C border to opposite sides of the A-B unit, again referring to Figure 1. Press seams toward borders.

3. Layer a backing square wrong side up and an insulating batting square. Center the pieced top right side up, on top of the batting and pin all layers together. Machine-topstitch around the edge of the embroidered square. Topstitch a second time ½ inch inside the first stitching, taking care not to stitch over the embroidered lines.

4. Repeat steps 1–3 for a second hot pad.

Thanksgiving Hot Pads
Placement Diagram 8" x 8" (includes binding)

Binding

1. Fold one binding strip in half along length wrong sides together; press.

2. Sew binding to hot pad edges starting at upper left corner, matching raw edges and mitering the three corners; stop after the third corner.

3. Trim off the excess backing and batting from the three stitched sides.

4. Starting in the upper left corner, fold binding to the back side and pin.

5. Finish sewing the binding on the last side and trim off the excess backing and binding.

6. Cut off binding 3½ inches from top edge of hot pad for loop.

7. Press under raw edge of loop ¼ inch and then bring the folded edges of loop together and stitch in place stopping about 1 inch from the hot pad as shown in Figure 2.

Figure 2

8. Insert end of loop into top binding seam as shown in Figure 3.

Figure 3

9. Hand-stitch the remainder of the binding and loop to finish.

10. Repeat to bind and add a loop to the second hot pad. ●

Autumn Table Runner

Bring plenty of seasonal color to your table while at the same time using up some of your fabric scraps.

Finished Size

71 x 15½ inches (excluding rickrack)

Materials

- 28 (2½ x 16-inch) print or tonal strips in a variety of autumn colors
- ½ yard cream solid
- Red embroidery floss (Cosmo #242 or DMC #498)
- Backing to size
- 1 yard 1⅜-inch-wide tan rickrack
- Thread
- Basic sewing tools and supplies

Cutting

From cream solid:

- Cut 2 (13 x 17-inch) rectangles.

Embroidery

1. Iron-on transfer or trace the autumn embroidery design in the center of each cream rectangle.

2. Embroider using two strands of floss, referring to Redwork Basics on page 3 as needed.

3. Press facedown on a terry towel to finish and trim each to 8 x 16 inches.

Assembly

Machine-stitch with right sides together using a ¼-inch seam allowance.

1. Join two print or tonal strips along length and sew to the long bottom edge of each embroidered panel; press seam toward strips.

2. Join remaining strips and add the embroidered panels to each end referring to the Placement Diagram. Press seams away from embroidered panels.

3. Cut rickrack into two 16½-inch pieces. Center the rickrack on the seam line at both ends, folding the raw edges of the rickrack under ½ inch so it will not be caught in the side seams as shown in Figure 1. Baste in place.

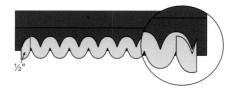

½"

Figure 1

4. Sew pieced top right sides together with backing, leaving a 6-inch opening on one long side for turning.

5. Turn runner right side out; press and stitch opening closed.

6. Machine-topstitch ⅛ inch around all four edges to finish. ●

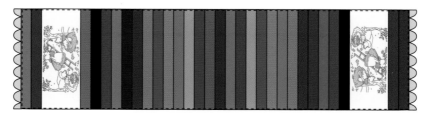

Autumn Table Runner
Placement Diagram 71" x 15½" (excluding rickrack)

Bread Bin

A bread bin helps to keep your bread warm. The top closes when the magnets on the handles are squeezed together. The optional bread warmer can be warmed in the microwave and placed in the bottom before the bread is added.

Finished Size

6¾ inches tall x 7 inches in diameter

Materials

- ⅜ yard cream solid
- ½ yard red print
- ¼ yard needle-punched insulating batting
- ½ yard extra-firm interfacing
- Red embroidery floss (Cosmo #2241 or DMC #816)
- 4 (½-inch) magnets
- Thread
- Basic sewing tools and supplies

Optional Bread Warmer

- 8 x 16-inch rectangle red print
- 8 x 16-inch rectangle batting
- ¾ cup uncooked rice

Cutting

From cream solid:

- Cut 2 (13 x 8¼-inch) rectangles.
- Cut 1 bread bin bottom using template provided.

From red print:

- Cut 2 (11½ x 7-inch) rectangles for lining.
- Cut 1 bread bin bottom using template provided.
- Cut 1 (5¼ x 22½-inch) strip for top band.
- Cut 2 (3 x 8¼-inch) strips for handles.

From needle-punched insulating batting:

Cut 2 (11½ x 7-inch) rectangles.
Cut 1 bread bin bottom using template provided.

From extra-firm interfacing:

Cut 2 (11½ x 7-inch) rectangles.
Cut 1 bread bin bottom using template provided.

From optional bread warmer materials:

Cut 2 red print and 2 batting bread bin bottoms using template provided.

Embroidery

1. Iron-on transfer or trace the wishbone embroidery design in the center of each cream rectangle.

2. Embroider using two strands of floss, referring to Redwork Basics on page 3 as needed.

3. Press facedown on a terry towel to finish and trim to 11½ x 7 inches.

Assembly

Machine-stitch with right sides together using a ¼-inch seam allowance unless otherwise indicated.

1. Layer one batting rectangle, one interfacing rectangle and one embroidered piece right side up; baste all edges using a scant ¼-inch seam for front. Repeat with remaining embroidered piece for back.

2. Sew the front and back with right sides together along sides; press seams open.

3. Mark the front and back centers with pins and set outer shell aside.

4. Layer bottom pieces of batting, interfacing and cream fabric right side up; baste together around outside edge using a scant ¼-inch seam.

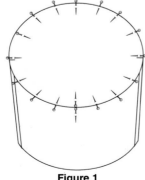

Figure 1

5. Sew the bottom to the outer shell with right sides together, matching centers and sides as shown in Figure 1. Turn right side out.

6. Sew the lining front and back together along sides; press seams open.

7. Sew the red print bottom to the lining front/back, matching centers and sides, referring again to Figure 1. Leave wrong side out.

8. Slip the lining piece into the outer shell, matching the side seams; baste top edges together.

9. Fold and press handles in half lengthwise.

10. Open handles, and then fold and press both raw edges into the center fold as shown in Figure 2. Bring both folded edges together, again referring to Figure 2; press and machine-topstitch along both edges.

Figure 2

11. Sew top band strip together on short ends; press seam open. Fold and press in half lengthwise.

12. Working from the outside of the bread bin, pin the raw edges of the top band to the top of the bread bin as shown in Figure 3. Sew band in place using a ¾-inch seam allowance. Press top band up.

Figure 3

13. Fold under ½ inch on both ends of each handle. Position each handle on the top band 2¾ inches from the side seam, keeping the handle even with the lower edge of top band as shown in Figure 4. Topstitch in place.

Figure 4

14. On the inside of bread bin, remove a bit of the basting just beyond the ends of each handle stitching and slip a magnet into the ¾-inch seam allowance behind the layer of lining fabric only as shown in Figure 5. Arrange the magnets so they stick to each other when the bag is closed. Stitch beside each of them to hold them in place.

Figure 5

15. Fold top band down to the lining side to cover seam allowance; hand-stitch in place.

Bread Bin
Placement Diagram 6¾" tall x 7" in diameter

Optional Bread Warmer

1. Sandwich both fabric bottoms with right sides together between the two batting bottom pieces. Machine-stitch together using a ½-inch seam allowance, leaving a 3-inch opening.

2. Turn right side out; press and fill with rice. Hand-stitch opening closed with a running stitch that can easily be removed to empty rice before washing as needed. ●

Front

Side

Side

Bread Bin
Bottom
Cut 1 cream solid
Cut 1 red print
Cut 1 interfacing
For optional bread warmer:
Cut 2 red print
Cut 2 batting

Back

Mug Rug

A mug rug is designed to hold your cup of coffee or tea with room on the side for a treat or snack. It's so much prettier than a napkin.

Finished Size

10½ x 6½ inches (including binding)

Materials

- 9-inch square white tonal
- ⅛ yard red tonal
- ¼ yard red print
- Red embroidery floss (Cosmo #346 or DMC #321)
- 1¼ yards ⅜-inch-wide white rickrack
- 10½ x 6 ½-inch rectangle batting
- Thread
- Basic sewing tools and supplies

Cutting

From red tonal:

- Cut 1 (2¼-inch by fabric width) strip for binding.

From red print:

- Cut 1 (4½ x 6½-inch) rectangle.
- Cut 1 (10½ x 6½-inch) rectangle for backing.

Embroidery

1. Iron-on transfer or trace the snowman embroidery design in the center of the white tonal square.

2. Embroider using two strands of floss, referring to Redwork Basics on page 3 as needed.

3. Press facedown on a terry towel to finish and trim to 6½-inch square.

Assembly

Machine-stitch right sides together using a ¼-inch seam allowance.

1. Baste a 6½-inch piece of rickrack centered on the seam line of the right edge of the embroidered square.

2. Sew the 4½ x 6½-inch red print rectangle to right edge of the embroidered square. Press seam toward the red fabric.

Mug Rug
Placement Diagram 10½" x 6½"

3. Center rickrack on seam line along the outside edges of pieced unit as shown in Figure 1 and baste in place.

Figure 1

4. Sandwich batting between the stitched top and the backing piece; pin or baste layers together to hold.

5. Fold binding strip in half with wrong sides together along length; press.

6. Machine-stitch binding to edges, matching raw edges, mitering corners and overlapping ends.

7. Fold binding to the back side and stitch in place to finish. ●

Gift Bags

Gift-giving is a joy with these versatile Sunbonnet Sue gift bags. They also work great as needlework bags.

Finished Size

9 x 11 x 4 inches

Materials

- ½ yard white solid
- ½ yard red-and-white print
- ½ yard red-and-green stripe
- 1⅝ yards iron-on, nonwoven firm interfacing
- Red embroidery floss (Cosmo #246 or DMC #321)
- 2⅝ yards ¼-inch-wide red rickrack
- 2⅝ yards ¼-inch-wide white rickrack
- 1¾ yards ⅜-inch-wide white rickrack
- Thread
- Basic sewing tools and supplies

Cutting

From white solid:
- Cut 1 (14-inch by fabric width) strip.
  Subcut into 4 (14 x 9-inch) rectangles.

From red-and-white print:
- Cut 2 (13½ x 16-inch) rectangles.

From red-and-green stripe:
- Cut 2 (13½ x 16-inch) rectangles.

From interfacing:
- Cut 4 (13½ x 16-inch) rectangles.

Embroidery

1. Iron-on transfer or trace the Nativity embroidery design in the center of two white solid rectangles.

2. Iron-on transfer or trace the gift-giving embroidery design in the center of the two remaining white solid rectangles.

3. Embroider using two strands of floss, referring to Redwork Basics on page 3 as needed.

4. Press facedown on a terry towel and trim each piece to 13½ x 6 inches.

Assembly

Machine-stitch right sides together using a ¼-inch seam allowance.

1. Press under ¼-inch on the top and bottom of each Nativity embroidered rectangle.

2. Iron an interfacing piece to the back of both red-and-white print bag pieces.

3. Machine-stitch an embroidered band to each bag piece, placing the band 4½ inches above the bottom of the bag as shown in Figure 1.

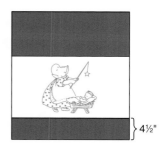

4½"

Figure 1

4. Cut four 15½-inch pieces from both the ¼-inch-wide red and white rickrack. Using one of each color, weave rickrack together as shown in Figure 2. Repeat to make four woven strips.

Figure 2

5. Stitch the rickrack trim on the top and bottom edges of the embroidered band by hand or by machine using a zigzag stitch and clear thread. Trim any excess rickrack.

6. Sew the bag pieces right sides together down the sides and across the bottom. Press side seams toward the front and the bottom seam toward the back.

7. With the bag still wrong side out, fold each corner so the side seam and bottom seam align. Mark a stitching line at a right angle to the seam and 2 inches from the corner point as shown in Figure 3. Stitch along the marked lines to form square corners.

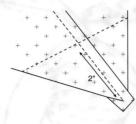

Figure 3

8. Press under the top edge of bag 2 inches toward interfacing side. Turn bag right side out.

9. Press bottom creases to make a flat bottom, going from corner to corner on all four sides as shown in Figure 4.

Figure 4

10. Press creases going up the side, 2 inches from side seam down to corners as shown in Figure 5.

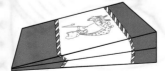

Figure 5

11. Cut two 13-inch pieces from both the ¼-inch-wide red and white rickrack. Using one of each color, weave rickrack together referring to Figure 2. Repeat to make two woven strips.

12. Fold both ends of each strip under ½ inch. To create handles, position woven rickrack on bag 2½ inches from each side crease and ¾ inch down from top as shown in Figure 6. Hand stitch in place.

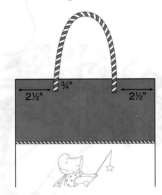

Figure 6

13. Repeat steps 1–12, skipping steps 4 and 5, to assemble second gift bag from striped fabric and using the gift-giving embroidery design and four 13-inch pieces of ⅜-inch-wide white rickrack for handles. ●

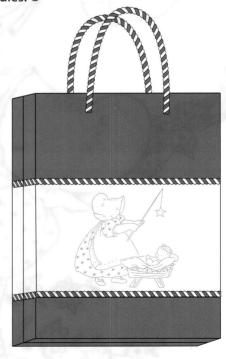

Gift Bags
Placement Diagram 9" x 11" x 4"

The Four Seasons

Spring Embroidery Design

Use for Tracing

The Four Seasons
Autumn Embroidery Design
Use for Tracing

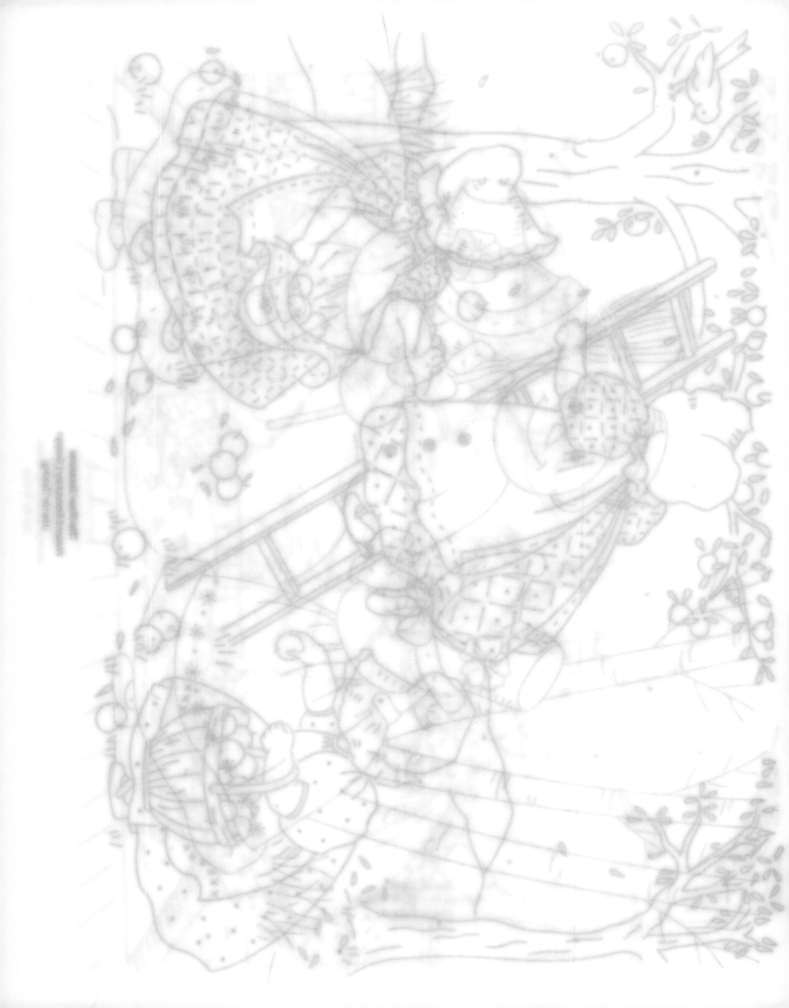

Easter Towels
Bunnies Embroidery Design
Use for Tracing

Easter Towels
Bird Embroidery Design
Use for Tracing

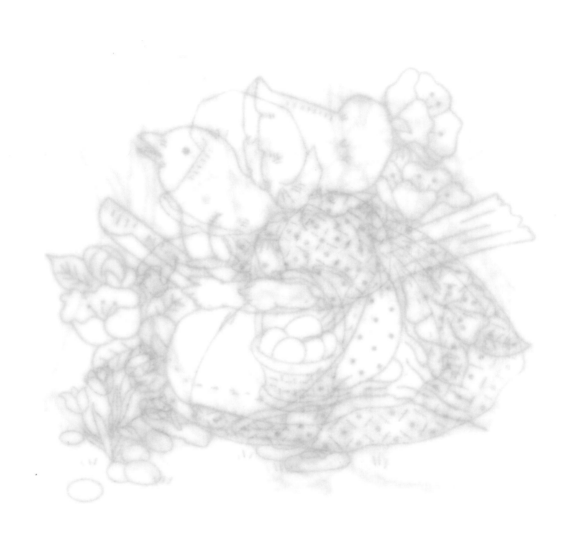

Easter Towels
Easter Eggs Embroidery Design
Use for Tracing

Halloween Pennant Banner
Pumpkin Carving Embroidery Design
Use for Tracing

Halloween Pennant Banner
Halloween Cat Embroidery Design
Use for Tracing

Halloween Pennant Banner
Scary Halloween Embroidery Design
Use for Tracing

Thanksgiving Hot Pads
Turkey Dinner Embroidery Design
Use for Tracing

Thanksgiving Hot Pads
Feeding Turkey Embroidery Design
Use for Tracing

Bread Bin
Wishbone Embroidery Design
Use for Tracing

Mug Rug
Snowman Embroidery Design
Use for Tracing

Gift Bags
Gift-Giving Embroidery Design
Use for Tracing

Gift Bags
Nativity Embroidery Design
Use for Tracing

The Four Seasons
Spring Embroidery Design
Use for Iron-On Transferring

The Four Seasons
Autumn Embroidery Design
Use for Iron-On Transferring

Easter Towels
Bunnies Embroidery Design
Use for Iron-On Transferring

TEST PATTERN

Easter Towels
Bird Embroidery Design
Use for Iron-On Transferring

TEST PATTERN

Easter Towels
Easter Eggs Embroidery Design
Use for Iron-On Transferring

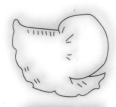

Halloween Pennant Banner
Pumpkin Carving Embroidery Design
Use for Iron-On Transferring

TEST PATTERN

Halloween Pennant Banner
Halloween Cat Embroidery Design
Use for Iron-On Transferring

TEST PATTERN

Halloween Pennant Banner
Scary Halloween Embroidery Design
Use for Iron-On Transferring

TEST PATTERN

Thanksgiving Hot Pads
Turkey Dinner Embroidery Design
Use for Iron-On Transferring

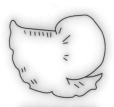

Thanksgiving Hot Pads
Feeding Turkey Embroidery Design
Use for Iron-On Transferring

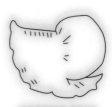

Bread Bin
Wishbone Embroidery Design
Use for Iron-On Transferring

TEST PATTERN

Mug Rug
Snowman Embroidery Design
Use for Iron-On Transferring

TEST PATTERN

Gift Bags
Gift-Giving Embroidery Design
Use for Iron-On Transferring

TEST PATTERN

Gift Bags
Nativity Embroidery Design
Use for Iron-On Transferring

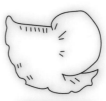

TEST PATTERN